Poetry's Poesy Vol. 2 Scattered Prayers

Brooks Crittenton

Royal Media and Publishing
P. O. Box 4321
Jeffersonville, IN 47131
502-802-5385
http://royamediaandpublishing.com
royalmediapublishing@gmail.com

© Copyright – 2021

All Rights Reserved. No part of this book may be reproduced, stored in a retrieval system, or transmitted by any means without the written permission of the author.

Cover Design: Gad Elite Book Covers

ISBN-13: 978-1-955501-00-2

Printed in the United States of America

Dedication

All I can say is thanks to The Most High, for being there even, when you didn't seem to be. The blessings & lessons of this year, I appreciate you.
This goes to my Tribal Family, the ones who been there through sunny days & the storms.
I Love You!!!

Table of Contents

Dedication	iii
Introduction	ix
Poesy	xi
Thank you Abba	1
Paean 1	2
Brooks Crittenton	**4**
Crittenton	4
Innocence	6
Paean 2	9
Paean 3	11
Paean 4	12
Paean 5	14
Paean 6	15
Broken Commitment	17
Iniquity	19
Paean 7	20
The Muses of Brooks	**21**

Rebekah	21
Paean 8	23
Running	24
Paean 9	26
Rachel	27
Deborah	29
Hagar	31
Real Me	33
Failed	35
Paean 10	36
I'm Coming	37
Homeless	**39**
Paean 11	39
Paean 12	40
Paean 13	41
Devil's Armpit	42
Paean 14	43
Paean 15	44
Paean 16	45
Myrrh	46

Paean 17	48
Paean 18	49
My Addiction	50
Paean 19	52
Fasting	53
Paean 20	53
Paean 21	54
That's All They See	55
Paean 22	58
Baptism	59
House of David	61
Lost Sheep	61
TLK	63
Paean 23	65
Paean 24	66
Paean 25	67
Was That You?	68
My Tribal History	70
My Family	74

Besties	**74**
Bruthas and Sistas	**75**
Paean 26	**76**
Goddaughters	**77**
Women of My Village	**78**
Nephews and Nieces	**80**
Royal Media	**81**
Your Vessel	**82**
Your Mercy	**84**
This Country (United States of America)	**86**
Covid-19	**88**
Politicians	**90**
My Leap	**91**

Introduction

Poetry's Poesy "Scattered Series" introduces "Scattered Prayers" the second volume. This volume continues to get in the mind of Poetry through prayers. Since the release of Poetry's "Scattered Thoughts" The Most High blessed his son by placing his book in a Black History Museum in East Point, GA on Juneteenth weekend of 2020. Wynn's Legacy House elevated the mind of Poetry, from East Point, GA Poetry traveled to Louisville, KY at the time of Ms. Breanna Taylor's death. While selling his first books hand to hand Poetry met a lot of amazing people. As this was going on Poetry's faith in The Most High was growing. Mistakes were made, placing dreams before his family. These are prayers from the fall of Brooks and the rise of TLK Poetry.

Through this journey Poetry ended up living in Las Vegas where battles he's faced, fighting the demons of his mistakes. Praise to The Most High, he's still here. As Poetry continues his journey, his Tribe is growing. Love & Blessings to all.

Such an amazing read.

Poesy

I've grown in your artform
I have given you my heart,
so, my old self will be reborn
The start was rocky,
mentors taught me
I've stumbled in this journey
I'm not perfect,
you instilled patience
I need it urgent,
tired of looking in eyes who's waiting
this platform, gave dream chasing
back breaking, mind shaking
You gave love when needed
You held my secrets
Offered tools to fight my demons
Poesy
I've grown in your artform
I have given you my heart,
so, my old self will be reborn

Thank you, Abba
For waking me up in the mornings
Blessing me even when I've proved nothing
Your loving & kindness is something
No matter the situation
I praise who You are.

Lord, wasn't it you who placed the stars?
I appreciate Your patience
As you had with Abram,
Your mercy is compared to no other.
I see the grace You give to my sisters and brothers
You are amazing in my sight.

It's frightening to think
How You look at me through Your sight
I fear Your might.
I praise You for being that Perfect Father,
I'm grateful for my Perfect Brother
Who walked on water.

Paean 1

I've longed for Your love
A spiritual being who cannot give hugs.
He is
My strength
My reach
My outreach to our wavelength.

You dusted me off
You love me
Yah, You're the only one who knows me
You know all my secrets
You know all my demons.
Yet still—
You talk to me
You saw those tears nobody would see.
Yet still—
You walk with me
You grip me tight.

When I have to walk these streets,
You give the Words.
When there're times I can't speak
Oh—You are there when…
Oh—You know that situation
I can't speak on that in this conversation.

Yet still—
You here with me.

It's funny:
I'm running to Your Word with wide open arms
I'm opening my ears, I can hear It
I can't explain Your Spirit
I appreciate Your grace
All I want
Is for You to smile on my face.

You know my low days
My sleazy ways
Yet still—
You show me a better me
A heaven where I would like to be
Looking down at Your feet
Waiting for you to speak.
Lord, where do you want me?

Crittenton

Brooks Crittenton

Brooks Crittenton must die!
Through his lips, he speaketh lies
That man was dirty in The Father's eyes
Not worthy
I broke those hearts
I wasn't sorry
Military action, doing my passion
I wasn't including You
Why?

I was up
Enjoying myself with liquor in my cup
I was by myself
You...somewhere on the shelf
Watching me be sneaky dream thieving
None of this bothered me

I was up
Then I fell
Lord, will You come help?
I put myself in this situation
If You help, I'll never do it again
He helps me out, and then I sin

Countless times, over, and over again
I broke laws, commandments
Every time He saw

Gave Him a simple repentance:
A lamb, such an infant
A man, let's get twisted
A Cain, excuses—I ain't perfect
Never admitting this world ain't working
Yet still, I'll live it
Never willing

I'm on this road alone with all this killing
There's murder on everybody's mind
Even hear it in the children
My eyes grew to see in the dark
Yet still, I would swim kuz she wanted me in.

I was up
This is MY increase
Spending it on unnecessary things
In my mind I'm a King
But...Brooks Crittenton must die
To understand what that means!

Innocence

He talks to those walls
Gypsum keeps him protected with his flaws
She wants to scream on what she just saw.
Innocence was confiscated
A whole mind frame was shaken
Being touched in private places
Doors locked—keys thrown away from this situation.

Those walls was trying to speak
On this old and young flirtation.
The old knew
Nobody wouldn't accept what the young was saying.
This child's mind was changing.
To his parents
His infatuation to this older woman
Was the strangest.

Her warmth was contagious
Her actions were heinous
Their relationship was wild
How this woman was loving this child.

Taking his shirt off, pulling his pants down
Carpet burns from the interaction on the ground.
She knew he wouldn't make any type of sounds
Kuz he's getting his manly lessons now.

Father laying many guidelines down
He is the man of his house
But doesn't notice what's going on
In his own background.
Corners mask this boy's noise,
While in the dark she plays with her new toy
Bringing light, he, experiencing a unique joy
Something special for him to enjoy.

This woman made the choice
He would be a playboy
Planting her seeds, growing his needs
Their loving was private
Such frequency was silent.
Under his parents noses
He was receiving sexual doses
Overdosing on sensual pleasure

Not realizing
They were affecting his future
relationships forever.

She knew this secret would be kept
Under his favorite cover
The ceilings knew better
Kuz this boy learned
Not to speak on his feelings—ever.

Paean 2

Please forgive me of my sins
Yet, I have slipped and fell
Time
And time
Again

Forgive me of the times I put my life in my hands
You are the Almighty
How amazing You found favor in me
Forgive me of my hate
You wake me up day after day
How dare I not be thankful for Your Grace
Throwing stones to the next
As if I slapped my Father in the face
Forgive me for knowingly and unknowingly
Willing to break Your Laws
As if there's no consequences
The Law was right there, I just didn't receive
You know I didn't read

Forgive me for being me
Forgetting through You, there's peace

Dishonoring my father and mother
Envying brothers
Lustful interactions with sistas
Forgive me for putting You under my needs
Forgive me of my greed
Them Judas ways
You were there for me
I turned my back and I betrayed
Lord, I am ashamed

Forgive me when times got hard
You were to blame
Not faithfully calling Your name
Forgetting Your name is above all thangs
Forgive my forefathers of doing the same

Forgive me for not knowing who I am
Israelite—Your offspring
The mountains will shake when we sing
My only purpose in life is to share Your light
Forgive the Israelites for their past doings
You are the only One we should be pursuing
Please forgive us of our sins

Paean 3

Thank you for my upbringing!
Waking up to my mother singing
Rejoicing in Your name
My father on the pulpit
Giving the congregation free game
Grandpa Pastor Ford, taught the Word was my sword
My grandmothers walked the life we strive for
They gave the heart to love my brothers and sisters more
I received an extended family
Mama Bykes scolding me, trying to love me
Pops educating, teaching
Thank You for this village who helped raise me
I know it wasn't easy

Paean 4

I realize my life without You
Means nothing
Without You in my life,
I have nothing!

I'm dirty and need to be washed clean
Your words have meaning
Tired of waking up out my sleep screaming
Can't shake the images when I was dreaming
You are the only One who can save me
The only One there when nobody is around me

No longer does earthly possessions impress me
When I rest, there's nothing I can bring with me
I want to be kneeling at your feet...
Patiently waiting Your command for me

Let my life be an extension of Your light
Remove my eyes
& lend me Your sight

Remove my ears
& lend me Your voice
So I can hear

Paean 5

Juneteenth—the wonders You did for me
Mrs. Wynn, presented legacy
In a house, where the tenants are history
I was not warned
My legacy would begin in the place I was born—
ATL, Georgia
Growing up in San Diego
I wanted to know Ya, know Ya
But I'm there
Dwelling amongst legends:
Laughing with Langston
Alex Haley standing
Martin thanking

The 1860s start speaking
"Poetry's Poesy"
Oh king, keep preaching
This bag on the wall starts coughing
Kuz it still holds original cotton
I sneak around the corner to see
John Hanson
My first president
Thank you, Yah
For making me a resident

Paean 6

Thanks for waking me up!
I appreciate my Big Brother for that blood in His cup
The reasons why I am not perfect
Is something I wouldn't want to discuss
You might look at my life in disgust
& look away

How do You look at my heart when I pray?
Didn't you see what I did the other day?
Can't be no way
You'll forgive me for the things I do
All I hear is pick up your feet and move—
To where?

Sometimes it's unbelievable,
Honestly incredible
Miracles in today's times
How can that be?
I mean for real...
How do You watch over me?
I was selfish with my needs
Concerns on greed.
Not on Your time, I was on mine

Living life on a thin line
You calling my name
I'm turning a blind eye
Who am I
To have the audacity, to turn on my Father
Only calling Him when times get harder?
Who Am I
To feel I'm owed?
My Father has no time for that on His throne!

There're too many problems going on
Instead of whiners
Souljas needs to be strong
Your grace, forgives my wrongs
Just You waking me up,
Encouraging me to move on
Amen

Broken Commitment

I DO
Supposed to protect you
Supposed to love you
Through sickness and hard times
Supposed to still rock with you
I played with vows
No walking down aisles
I didn't bring smiles
No excuse
I didn't know how to resist
A pretty face was my weakness
Especially if she insist
Whispering she wants to know me
Her touch was a reflection
Opposite of the at home stressing
Her touch was a self-reflection
Of what I was missing

I DO
Supposed to not forsake
Supposed to not throw dirt in your face
How could I?
When I'm was still learning life
Reflecting on myself and judging my wife
Disrespecting oneself and

Not treating you right
How could you not do this to I?
I work
I try
I slip
I lie

I DO
Want you to come over one more time
I want us to end on a good note
As we write on these dangerous lines

I DO
Know you...
Addictive
Deceitful
Untruthful
Lustful
Toxic
Extramarital
Relations
Yielding
YOU ARE...ADULTERY!

Iniquity

I have died in these sins
Lord be merciful when You punish me
There's no excuse for why I would keep doing it again
I know You've already forgiven
Still, I have to walk this sentence, period!

MY FATHER loves me unconditionally
But breaking His laws
Those crimes are serious
Waking up from escaping those demons
Knowing the meaning
It was always—
My free will
Yet, I caused these situations on the real

No excuse!
I was taught in my youth
Since then, Brooks showed
He would do what he wanna do
No matter who I hurt in the process too
Intentionally and unintentionally
I was learning me

Paean 7

I've been washed before
& that was a long time ago
I wanna be clean
Letting go of past things
For Him I'm learning to sing
He walks with me
& sees what I see
Dirty or clean

The Muses of Brooks

<u>Rebekah</u>

Lord, I got to experience love
Young, naive you wouldn't believe how deep
Sneaking sometimes to meet.

Many first—my first.
Please forgive the times I brought hurt
No matter what, we were going to work.
We were fools
We broke rules
We chased truth.
I slipped
I tripped
I didn't know what to do.
Yah, I kept messing up, I had to move
I put this on You.

My beloved, we loved
You were everything to me
The seed was planted.
We was gonna be a mighty tree
Producing our fruit, I was tarnishing the hue.

Looking in your eyes,
I couldn't face my wrongs
I couldn't hold on—made myself move on

I acknowledge.
I left home, she bore Knowledge
Learning many lessons
She was love.
For that family
Keep sending Your blessings
From the throne above.

Paean 8

Yah
I still think of her
She in my dreams
She in my nightmares
She still is here
But she still is there
This was my doing
I still love her
My family
My first
My…
Guide my heart and
Show me where to start

Running

Why do I run from her?
Every time I get a chance—I run
These years without her hasn't been fun.
Lord, only you know what I have done
I turned on You so I couldn't face her.

I ran as far as I could go.
I gave other women her seat
A stature they couldn't reach.
She's a part of me
We knew it would always be.

It was supposed to be
Printed in permanent ink
I rest on her name when I sleep
Or
On the date it became We.

Why do I run from her?
I'm not who I used to be
Will she see ME or me?
Would she see a king or a thrown away thing?
How could she know?

Through all these years she's been with me.
As I was learning,
I couldn't keep stringing her along
I was wrong.

Paean 9

Father,
I wanna be her man again
I don't think You understand
I came from the forbidden lands
Jungles with the contraband
Places where I forgot The Man
YOU!

You know The Man
He found me on these deathly lands
& lent me a helping hand.
You keep showing me love
Why these things keep happening,
It's crazy!
Our vocabulary never said, maybe
My demons never made you question,
Your baby.

On Thanksgivings you made it amazing
I was skating on anything that was hating
You holding on to my hand saying greatness
This union only happened kuz He made it.

Rachel

Most High,
Rachel came second
In our short time she showed blessings.
She was older, showed order
What a mother would do for her daughter
A panda low-key lacking a father.

I told Rachel,
"Get on this carpet,
I'll take you away from these lands
To foreign lands
I know how to be a man."
Without You in my life Lord,
I didn't understand.

Responsibility came, once before me.
I need to make sure they eat,
Rachel's father would teach.
Just like the first,
He said Your Word I should seek.

Rachel was so beautiful to me
Her voice made my soul sing.
To her, I wanted to be everything.
Watching musicals on TV

With a li'l beautiful flower next to me.

I became stronger but fell weak.
How can I do this to another family?
Rachel and I knew I wasn't ready
Leaving that home was unforgetting
In my mind unsettling.
Father have mercy
Look at my heart
& understand why I say bless 'em.

Deborah

I was in the land of the cardinal bird
In a place I needed a nurse
I met Deborah; she was my first judge

A line signed for militia,
This was our only move
She was learning her army
I was living with my karma
Fighting with a commander, in my own home

There was love there, somewhere
Natural hair, natural beauty
At times very soothing
Her daughter and me chilling
Lord, You know how she was
Oh, how You gave such a judge
She would give praise just because
Not afraid to tell me what it was

We were strong, then we had to split
I grew weak
They came by and gave me strength
It lasted a bit
The battle came

& I was ready to quit

Deborah, I apologize
I initiated the first strike
I just didn't know
Hers would be twice the might

Father, I looked in her eyes
& I saw my own life
I had to leave to make me right
For her many taught lessons
Please always guide her life

Hagar

I understand her anger
To me we were personal
To the outside she was a stranger
She was there through my wives
Someone to call during my hard times
So many times you blew my mind
You picked me up and dusted me off every time
Loyalty between me and you was no lie
Hagar, you saw the king before I could see
Father, forgive me for stringing her along
I fell in love with our song

Oh, how we made love
Samson strength to break tiles
I want my son right now...
She can't reach wife,
She knows this is not right
To deny her was an impossible fight
I apologize, for any contribution of pain
Every time we come around each other, There's no gain
This was toxic, I had her dazed
I'm not perfect
Never expected for things to go this way

I pray for You to guide her steps
She still loved me
When she was the last left
Stay close to her children
Lord be the ointment to their healing

Real Me

I am man, I'm not perfect
I fight these humanly urges
You were all worth it
We prayed before we went to sleep
I appreciate, that y'all kept me in my Word
You never shunned me, even though I was dirty

Y'all forgave me
Y'all loved me
Y'all came through
Y'all showed me
You know where we met, you felt His energy
I wanted you safe with me
My Father, watch over their family...
You smile on relationships done right
I think about y'all at night

Rolled my blunts
& used to wonder how our numbers were aligned
Life got really hectic
The enemy was very disrespecting

I didn't know how to keep on stepping
I was always forgetting
It was Him
Who's always getting me out my messes

Failed

Father, I failed
It was the flesh again
Such a battle with the pleasures within
Some battles concerning Your law,
I was winning
Then I slipped and fell in a sundress.

You of all people know it wasn't on purpose
Business was being handled on the surface
Words were being written
Drinks we started sipping
Forgive me of my blurred vision
Because of that bath—*I mean*—backroom
I went in
I can't lie
The eye contact was locked on.

When I crossed the threshold,
That grip became really strong
It was mutual
Forgive me of my actions
Since I fell in passion.

Paean 10

Watch over their tribes, Lord
Their families & more
Their parents who would still guide me
They had beautiful spirits
You can feel it
My in-laws are blessed by my Father
Their brothers, their sisters, and children
Keep Your hands over them
Guide 'em as they walk
A strong melanin family
When I was younger, they kept me in church
Making sure I constantly heard Your word

I'm Coming

So sexy—such a beauty
What your smells will do,
When you are next to me.
Why can I not get to this lady?
Just the thought drives me crazy!
Such a flower, so delicate
At this moment, I'm not able to represent.

I yearn.
Every day I learn a little more of the definition of love.
My beloved
I'll wait for you
Maybe one of the lamest things
My brothers would say I could do.
I'll wait for you
Experiences you will bring will be new,
My past won't matter to you.

All my beloved will see is me
A man in stature, she couldn't believe.
Next will come an embrace that will be unforgetting
Love will be made, without them knowing each other.

Soft touches, light kissing
Leaving each other missing
Their energy.
She will claim he is clean
He will wash the dirt,
So he can be with she.
How, woman, may my lips taste
something so sweet?

I'll wait for—WE.
Let me dip in this water to be clean for
our team.
As my queen, let's conquer these dreams
Teaching our generations how to believe.
My future
You will be so sexy, such a beauty,
You wouldn't believe
What your touch will do to me.

Homeless

Paean 11

I've served this country
Why am I homeless?
I provided for a family
Why am I homeless?
Everything was taken from me
No place to call home when I sleep
There's no excuse
That would be accepted from me
Boy, you know you strong
How do you just fall off?
It's not that hard to get a job
Or
Be like Job & know
Through all this
There is a story to be told

Paean 12

There is peace in Your name
I acknowledge this change
I can admit I don't want to be the same

Some things I've done I was ashamed
Why, I've done all my dirt in Your face
The secrets I did when I was in my own space
You were there

In a sense I did not care
Me, having to walk perfect in Your Word
In this world, I thought was not fair
Questioning You: Why am I here?

As I panic
He keeps me still
His voice is clear
The love is real
Your awesomeness
I fear
Yet,
There is peace in Your name

Paean 13

Thank you for feeding me every day
Providing my needs in every way
No money in my pocket
Still, He fills
Home cooked meals
Drinks to sip
Herb ready to be lit
On a daily I receive a gift
I learn from Your creation
I converse with Your creation
Creatures know I have dominion
Yet, I learn how to be so free
The birds aren't concerned how they're going to eat
How can they be smarter than me?
Forgive me when I doubt
Every time You show up with a feast

Devil's Armpit

I don't like what I see
So many people in need
Lord protect those in these streets
I want to help but they are the same as me
This road goes deep
So many souls, this is where they sleep
This armpit is not where You want them to be
Father help them get free
They need love just like me

Paean 14

Oh, how they look at me
In a community where they see me dirty
Sleeping in a city of sin
Falling for temptation again
Oh, why do I let the Devil win?
Why do I fall?
When I've been taught to stand tall
You are who I call

Paean 15

You are love
& love is You
I call to You
& have to push on through
You are love
This feeling is new
I took on Your Word
& hold it true

Paean 16

You blessed us with a new year
The last put me in my feels
I couldn't believe it was real
I knew I was weak—boy was looking ill
Yah, I seen Your light,
Your peace made my heart alright
Looking for approval in Your sight
Through You I can reach any heights...

Thank You for blessing us with a new year
I pray You look over the one's still here
If anybody lost someone last year
Due to the pandemic, Lord wipe their tears
For Your children, block their fears
We praise You, kuz we got to see a new year

Myrrh

I light
"What does it do?"
Gives sight
"To what?"
My might
I respect the herb
It connects me with Word
Relatable in today's world

I'm lit
I got this as a gift
In my accounts I have no cents
I get to light
I read
I write
It calms my mind, I'm with You this time
You know Your son loves this flower
The benefits—the power

I don't really crave to eat
Rather would like Your company around me
You show my ways, we have them days
I get that gram, You make sure I'm okay
Sometimes two, or I get the eighth

He keeps His son straight
Your time, I don't want to waste
This knowledge I chase

Paean 17

Father have mercy on my soul
There are things I do not know
Forgive me for times when I bring up the Word
& there's frustration in our conversation
When I speak of Thee,
There should be peace
Sometimes that's not the case
I feel different energy,
Not how it supposed to be
Just trying to express what You have done for me
This transformation was unseen,
Without too much knowledge of the Bible
Those Words are exciting
When in real time you see the blessings
He is a Father, there comes many lessons
Father have mercy on my soul
For the things I did not know

Paean 18

You gave tools to speak
Dreams to reach
Mapped out a road
I just didn't know the length
My mother prayed for my strength
There's so much Samson in me
The weakness to women
Telling 'em my secrets
Until it comes back to me
I'm battling the army all by myself
I know I can't make it; really need Your help
You sat me down, when there was no one left
You showed me right and let me step left

My Addiction

Our first interaction was under blankets
Back then I was just playing
I remember my first hit
I was in a hallway
I needed more of this
I'm doing this all the way

The feeling was great
Lying on the ground in an uncommon place
Why every time we meet,
You have a different face?
Say when, I'll make a way

That night of my graduation
Those wives gave a celebration
In the next room, laid my grandma
After the sheep, she slept
Towels under the bathroom door,
This fun can't make it through those walls
I was in too deep

More in my addiction I crept
It consumed, the reason for my fall
This I must reap, that's why my soul wept

Father, You kept me safe
Even when I was in my own ways

This drug I needed all the time
Twenty-four-seven always playing in my mind
I feel nervous, I'm about to relapse
You greet with a smile on the surface,
Who seems koo and relaxed
Lord, only You can help with this addiction

I love the touch of the dealers
When I'm off balanced, they my healers
Hold my hand in this affliction
I no longer know what's real
No longer am I able to feel
I've grown numb every time I succumb
Asking for help because You're the only One

Paean 19

Thank You for another day to see:
Holidays
Birthdays
Worst days
Best days.
No matter what I lay at Your feet,
You make a way.
These are some of the reasons I pray.

Fasting

Paean 20

I'm being tempted
Battle after battle I can admit this
Lord, look at my heart
You knew the intention from the start
I'm in Your Word
Not caring on what I just heard
It's You and me now
I'm coming as a humble servant
With my head bowed

Paean 21

Distractions are around me
My urges make it hard to sleep
I'm getting hungry
Father I need something to eat
My mind gets fed
He fills me up
Without bread

Fasting

That's All They See

Black man, Black man
That's all they see
I'm a homeless man, writing in these streets
Harassed by security and police
I'm in a place I'm supposed to be
This situation could be the end of me

This lady getting out the car looks scared of me
Don't even want to know why she asks for I.D.
I have a warrant from years ago
She walks back to the car, and closed the door
I write this poem kuz I don't know how this can go
I'm in a place I'm supposed to be
This is where I'm at every day
This is where I'm free

Black man, Black man
That's all they see
What a surprise, she don't believe me

I was just on the phone with my brother
Corey
I spoke this might be
I just told him
If anything happens to me
Look after my moms

This police lady's voice just raised
I've served this country
She don't hear what I say
Don't move—just write—account your life
Her voiced just raised
I know someone in this place
She don't hear what I say

I pack my bags
I pray
I look at her
I walk away
I feel her car behind my feet, I pray
Today the devil been trying me, I pray
She's following; I'm walking, I pray
Sirens I hear, sirens I hear
They getting closer
I have a warrant
I have no fear, I pray

I walk a little further, then look back
Where is she?
The sirens just ceased
I walk, I sit, open my bag
& finish

Jesus, You really have me
My Big Brother
You're always there for me
Five more days before I get in the water
So He'll know me
His son, Poetry

Paean 22

One more day
I can't wait
You protect me in these ways
To dip in the water
When times get harder
I read Your Word
I get smarter

One more day
Until I'm clean
You had me safe, through those things
No longer restless when I wake
I hear the birds when they sing
The joy in their voice makes me read
What we went through
You made me believe
After tomorrow I'll be a child You see
Thank you for everything!

Baptism

All I want, is for You to smile
I landed safely
Time to hit those miles
Driving, surviving, trying
Lord thank You for protecting my journey
You taught me with no money

Question asked:
How are you going to get there?
My response—He will be there
A car out of thin air, gets me there
I'm aware
You are the only One I fear
Your perfection is the reason I'm here

We sung our songs
The journey to You was a little long
Your Words randomly coming from my phone
This mind is clean
I need the rest to be
From now on, I'm listening to You to guide me

Such a church, I had to walk through those doors
Knowing when I come out, I won't be the same no more
I spoke
In a room by myself
Clothes of my old self hit the floor
I'm in white
That step was cold
My spiritual advisor's praying
Father guide me where You want me to go

Under that water I went
Coming up thanking You
Is the only thing I find myself saying
It was cold—I didn't care
Kuz I felt YOU there
Brooks Crittenton is no longer
Through You I will be stronger

House of David

Lost Sheep

Yah, I'm a lost sheep from the house of David
There's no longer pastures or grazing
I need my Shepherd
For these dangers I'm facing
Tripping, second guessing
Why do I do such things when You are amazing?

I'm a lost sheep, from the house of David
History of royalty
As a lamb my mother told me these things
I was curious, distractions were everything
Had no time to stop, looking up I lost my flock
Dangers I feared, kuz I didn't feel You here
Deep inside I knew You were near
So how dangerous can this life be
When I heard the promises
Which was given to me

I come from the same house where rocks are thrown
Heads cut off domes for disrespecting He

We should strive to be just
With my brothers, my language is trust
His daughters I try not to fall in lust
Break me of my ways of human
Breathe in me what you want me doing
I trust You in all my movements
This mustard seed, help me free
Something so small, help me see
I'm a lost sheep from the house of David

TLK

I AM THE LAST KING
Yah, protect my heart
Be the ointment on my scars
When I look in the mirror, I see You
David, Samson, Saul
You gave me the strength to knock down any walls
My Father's grace keeps my head tall
Guide me during this spiritual warfare
My enemy is in the midst, I feel him near
Lurking, working
He's real
I'm armed with no steel

I AM THE LAST KING POETRY
Teach me to act as such
Your laws are just
Your Word I trust
When I had nothing
You filled my cup
This crown that rests on my head is not mine
I seek no recognition in my eyes
I'm only a lion watching over his pride

When You roar through me, the ground starts shaking
You open my heart to witness
Your amazement
I appreciate this seat
In this lineage of royalty
But know me as Your humble servant
Diligently working on Your purpose
That battlefield no longer has me nervous

I praise Your name
My walk done changed
I ask You to be the head over my reign
THE LAST KING POETRY...
I Am grateful for this given name

Paean 23

I pray for guidance
No longer am I an adolescent
Afraid to ask a question
Or ask for protection.
Guide me to share Your light
Through my life
PLEASE!

Guide me to share Your light
Through my imperfect life.
See...
Just a while ago I was in HELL so,
I had to replace the H with a Y
For me to YELL!
H ran to imperfect
My yelling finally reached Him.
He split to go handle some business,
But left His perfect grace for His children.

Paean 24

Glory to Your name
You love me all the same
I walked in Your house
They started to praise
She hit that chord
My tears started to pour
The message was clear
You were speaking in my ear
You shielded me through this last year

Glory to Your name
You know my name
You took my shame
You Love me all the same
I just want to please You in all my ways
I walked in Your House
& I had to praise
In foreign lands,
You held my hand
Constantly stumbling on Your road
Still trying to achieve Your goal
My Almighty Father
You never abandoned me
When times got harder

Paean 25

Though I walk through the valley of the
shadow of death
I try not to fear no evil
I smell his breath
Can feel devilish ways,
Amongst some of these people.
The air is foul
On this land I prowl
Around these towns
Searching for my lost lineage crown

As I trek through this valley
My Father keeps safeguarding
The Father of Abraham loves me
regardless
He always keeps food on my plate
There's no obstacle too great
You know the things I faced
Yet still I'm here in this deathly place
Reaching for Your grace
Accepting my humanly mistakes
Appreciating You love me this way

Was That You?

Did I meet You last night?
Did I get a chance to see You last night?
Was I tripping?
Kuz I know I wasn't drinking last night
Your presence brought a calmness
In a place where it's not the calmest

Do you know who I am?
The only thing the man asked
Before I was grabbed
In the midst of all the noise
I had to rejoice
Mention my Father's name
He is not here for no type of game
He loves me for who I am
In the midst of all the madness
My attention's to You
How did You grab it?
It had to be You there
I felt Your breath in the air
In a crowd of despair
For a split second did I see Your face?
Working on a daily just for Your grace
Your smile is bright on my face
Was I blessed to see You in that place?

Where the dead is awake?

My Father, just know I'm with You all the way
Forgive me of my past ways
I'm asking, Yah
Did I get a chance to meet You last night?
So, I can look in Your eyes
& know everything will be alright

My Tribal History

February 2021
I'm blessed to see another one—
Black History Month
A time to dwell on our history
They taught Malcolm, Rosa, Martin Luther King
Thurgood, Carver, and slavery

I used to tell 'em I love poetry
Alexander Pushkin
In the classrooms, they didn't teach
One of the greatest in Russia
And he looks like me
He wrote poesy like me
His great-grandfather
Abram Petrovich Gannibal:
A man in a high place
A General
We have the same face
An engineer with African origins
From Africa to Russia they sold 'em
Why do you not teach me
Of the man in the high place?
A General
We have the same face

This year I'm going to appreciate my history
The ones who laid down guidelines
To personally protect me—my tribal family
To understand the beginning of my history
You have to open that book and read
The blessings trickled down
To greats before me
Respecting our antiquity promises
Our grandparents had their children
Walking history in our village

Doctor's, millionaires, dentist
Business owners, CEO's, chemist
Militant, brilliant, resilient
A village of melanin-ation
Parents teaching us elevation
This is my village
If some provoked—they hittas
Some can lay hands on you—they healers
This is my village

As much history in my background,
Lord I'm privileged
Those children had kids

Them my cousins, brothers, and sisters
They showed us somethings whether
It was good, bad, or indifferent
Trying to teach us better

Our history is that Word
We were taught how to use that sword
My family is the real Israel
Chasers of God
My family cut, my village is strong
They the type to beat any odds
Our lineage taught the men in the village
How to stand tall
If we fall, we don't stay down long

The women in our village
Encourage us to be strong
Always those right words to help us move on
Our grandparents had their children
We come from those children
Walking history in my village
Nurses, students, artists
Workers, cooks, attendants
Activists, preachers—the few out the billions
Our village is of melanin-ation

Elders teaching us our nation
This is my village

There's some that know no filter
Some teachers teach us to be leaders
This is my village
The one's who passed down,
Guidelines to protect me and love me
This is my tribal history

My Family

Besties

Keep your arms around my besties
The two that would watch over me
This didn't have to be
They could have ignored me
They're the reason I have a high school degree
Sometimes in the morning they would feed me
Two angels to watch over he

Protect their families
Guide their husbands
They deserve to be treated right
Their small gesture saved a life
Watch over their children
I pray they keep You first

Bruthas and Sistas

Guide my bruthas and sistas
Through their journey
You know how much they mean to me
Place their feet in the right direction
Some of them are nice
Some will take a life, and you'll never see them again

Lord, You know the struggles we been through
We were taught to keep on moving
I apologize for my mistakes
Throwing their advice in their face
Most High, I want all my bruthas and sistas great
In this bloodline You gave
No matter what, they love me anyway
Please keep every single one safe
For them I'll chase Your grace
Our parents taught us You are the only way

Paean 26

I appreciate the times
Y'all check me when I'm out my mind
I really hear y'all at times
Y'all want the best for me
We check adversity, we're strong
Such audacity, you speak on our wrongs
We of flesh but have the capacity
Our life's a song—not of blood—we're family
You had us all along
I pray for everyone who's in this circle
Let them come out on top through any hurdle
The Almighty can fulfil any miracle

Goddaughters

To my goddaughters
I was chosen to be your godfather
For different reasons
It was your parents' decision.

Lord give me the strength to help raise
These beautiful children.
Your godfather will have your back 100%
No matter what it is.
Until I have no breath, I will always be here.
Father with these three, please stay near.
When they get older teach them to hear,
So they could see their purpose clear.

Women of My Village

Women of value who taught their children
Women of all ages, different classes
These are the women in my village
Melanin-ated, powerful, brilliant
None give up in my circle
They show their strength
Through their hurdles
Since birth, other women of the village
Would help my parents raise me
Adopting me in their families

Lord, they knew I was crazy
Like Mary, my bloodline come from that lady
I appreciate every single one of y'all
Many hands on my back, keeping me up tall
Still there with comfort when I fall

Lord, I don't know who I would be
Without these women who help guide me.
Father smile on all the women in my village
Have mercy and bless their children

Show them they're important in their lineage
I love all the women in my village

Nephews and Nieces

Nephews and nieces,
Y'all my heart.
It gets hard to love y'all from afar
These last years, your uncle fell hard
Not listening to grandparents,
Your parents, trying to help their brother.

For my nephews and nieces,
I'll pick up all the pieces.
There's no excuse
Your uncle always had a reason.
I see your parents in y'all eyes
Each one of y'all will be alright.
Y'all was born to a noble family
When you get older learn your history.
We come from royalty,
So always act accordingly.
All my nephews and nieces
Are blessed from head to feet.

Royal Media

You found royalty
When the average couldn't see
Such a platform for me
Given from He

Mrs. Julia published the skill
Lord she made the dream real
I was stressing, they said try and be still
You blessed me with a publishing company
That doesn't tax
From the beginning
A publishing family who has my back
When I'm wrong they tell me-like that
Royal Media seen a king
Named Poetry

Oh how much they will always mean to me
Father, they never did Your son wrong
Your name is glorified,
Their fruits please multiply

Your Vessel

I was always scared to be Your vessel
Letting Your Word flow
I felt I could never put them together
Staying away from You, I used effort
You pushed, nonetheless
For even me I'm impressed
Working seven days a week—365
You gave no rest
For years, I still gave less
Especially when your son was stressed

I was always scared to be Your vessel
I could never be perceived as holier-than-thou
When I'm still writing my wrongs down
My humanly needs weak
Your name at one point was hard to speak
I felt ashamed as if You wouldn't want me
How you wanted me to be
I thought it was impossible to reach
So, why not do me—
At least I'll feel free
Do as I please
Standing in these streets screaming
Only God can judge me

I took that in and for sure it scared me
How would He judge my life
While I've been me
Living this life without He?
My Father, the One who knew me
Before my mother got to hold me
I got lost in this world and forgot our intimacy
By the time I realized,
Your laws were foreign to me

I was always scared to be Your vessel
Some of Your angels I wrestled
Leaving their soul restless
I keep hearing You
Calling my name
This time, the tone in my voice
Was no game

Your Mercy

Walking on the street as the cars go by
I lift my head and look to the skies
A thought crossed my mind
As human beings, we shouldn't be alive
Didn't we take His only begotten Son?
Ask any parent, you take their children—
What they doing?
Whole families could get wiped out in one movement
But my Big Bro asked for mercy
We should be thankful for that doing
His Mercy keeps our mind
My Big Bro walked that perfect line
I'm the one that keeps messing up,
Slipping up
Yet, still I'm following behind
No, I'm far from perfect
Your mercy keeps serving
You know my heart
You keep me working
You gave us free will to keep searching
You gave me strength to fight some hurdles
Ask my brothers of my dirt,

In a drop of a dime, I'm down for any work
Your hands kept me safe, on the road
Your grace is protecting my way
Until I reached Your place
When I seen You, tears poured down my face
Even after that, I made mistakes
For my family, more risk I had to take
I didn't ask, I just went
In other idols I would vent
Came at a cost, trust I spent
Over, over, and over again
Your mercy picked me up again
Brushed me off and asked if I'm ready to win

This Country (United States of America)

Lord protect your people in these lands
We strive and we work as hard as we can
This country was built off the backs of man
Our women and men
Such ones that would look like me
My father and my mother….
The ones begotten before 'we'
I know you've heard our screams
You've seen our cries
We've said we tried
My brother understands our pain
Lord, we live in a country who uses Your name in vain

In our pledge of allegiance
We say "under God "
My leadership in this government
I don't see You at all
In God we trust
They slapped that on our currency
Deceitful transactions between us
THEY forgot those words, Your meaning
Father have mercy on Your people in these foreign lands

If You did it once, You'll do it again
With this land
As You will
Touch Your people's hearts
Keep their peace still
Only through You
Can we heal
Can we build
Your Grace is real

Covid-19

I rebuke you
It touched close ones.
My family:
Grandfathers, fathers, mothers, sisters, sons
A plague made by man's hand
So much killing
Most High, shield Your children
Covid-19 has no dominion over me
It is You who is watching over 'we'

Please hear our cries
Expose the lies
Help us dry our eyes
Lord, You are doing things
Even the virus couldn't see
Sprouting from underneath kings and queens
Following our God-given dream
Your blood is over my family
Covid-19 has no dominion over me
It is He who is watching over 'we'

Such a plague I thought I would never see

I read on death, but this will not have a sting on me
Lord, I have no fear
That's how You would like me to be

Politicians

I see them on TV
Making life decisions for 'we'
Most times their eyes show greed
No longer for the people's needs
Swearing to an oath they don't mean
Bills being passed
For the right amount asked
Lord not everyone should be corrupt
This country done had about enough
I pray these people have our best interest
When they pass around our lives
Deciding if they want to sign those lines
Due to the underlines
The things not seen on a TV screen
Touch their heart, tear the wicked apart
Guide their decisions amongst these men and women
The President, the Congress, these politicians
Father be there when they speak on our needs
Their pledge of allegiance, this oath is to You
Show us their hearts, so we'll know who to hold true.

My Leap

Lord help me hear You when You speak
If I can't move, help me move my feet
Believe me
Putting Your faith in Him is not easy
Why would it be?
My Brother had to suffer
What excludes 'we'?
Do we feel better than He?
What holds you back from the leap?